PAST DUE NOTICES

Poems 1991-2011
by
Mike James

[signature]
5-10-2014

MAIN STREET RAG
PUBLISHING COMPANY
Charlotte, North Carolina

Acknowledgments

Poems, or versions of these poems, have appeared in the following magazines and newspapers:

Abbey, Lummox Journal, Pittsburgh City Paper, 5 AM, Dufus, Philadelphia Poets, Motel 58, Bathtub Gin, The Main Street Rag, Charlotte Poetry Review, Iodine Poetry Journal, Laughing Dog Review, Pittsburgh Post-Gazette, Free Fall, Mobius, Buffalo Carp, Hot Metal Press, Poem, Poesy, Black Buzzard Review, Fight These Bastards, Skidrow Penthouse, Concho River Review, Muse & Stone, The Silt Reader, Pulp, Nerve Cowboy, and *Bumble Jacket Miscellany.*

"Poem Dictated at Kazansky's Deli" appeared in the anthology *Along These Rivers.*

"Necessary Fictions" appeared in the anthology *The Working Poet.*

Many of these poems were previously collected in the following collections:

Not Here (Green Bean Press, 2000), *All Those Goodbyes* (Talent House Press, 2001), *Pennies From An Empty Jar* (Another Thing Press, 2002), *Nothing But Love* (Pathwise Press, 2004), *Alternate Endings* (Foothills Publishing, 2007), *Shotgun Exchanges* (Costmary Press, 2010)

A line in the poem, "Jack Wolford" was taken from a poem by Kevin Cantwell.

Library of Congress Control Number: 2012935434

ISBN: 978-1-59948-354-2

Produced in the United States of America

Main Street Rag
PO Box 690100
Charlotte, NC 28227
www.MAINSTREETRAG.com

For Diane

Contents

The Limits

> *her foot-touch*
> *The place itself*
>   —James Dickey

The waves more expansive
than breath. We move on.

She brings me here
when darkness is half over
to watch against the tide.
The sand coarse as sea grass
against our feet.

In early autumn
we are not beneath any pier.
The driftwood stored for carving.

Our toes leave
only the slur of a print.
Walking, every grain returns,
like salt and bread
a beginning.

Swimmers, Just Married

we swim and find our bodies full length

wine drunk, we are interrupted
when a catfish jumps near us   we laugh

our mouths take in the wet moon
fallen upon the water

so many days without rain   the lake low
the water still clear

days without anger   the sleep-smile
of the first married

this is the beginning to all fairy tales
all we ever learn

Empty House: A Meeting Poem

nothing but sunlight and dust
to love in
we lie on the hardwood
awake

our fingers move slightly
a prayer of hands

wind blows through
a crack
in the window

the curtains
dirty bandages

we have almost forgotten
our life

Instructions to the Artist

Nothing is gained by assurance.
                    —Ted Berrigan

Get a dog that is friendlier than people…
      feed him bacon scraps &
      tell him your worst jokes.
Have a head that is harder than the shitheads
      that surround you.
Buy all your books second hand.
Buy a plant…a cactus, preferably,…or a loving fern.
Be like Bukowski & drink almost anything.
Rent a house with many windows.
Be like St. Francis & drink only water.
Count out the steps to the closest source of light.
Save all the letters you receive, let them be a constant,
      a journal of all that you know.
Read the comics while in the bathtub.
Be both ordinary & mystic.
Think, when you are walking, about how your legs feel…
      study the ease of a lazy man.
Live by eating leftovers from the refrigerators of friends.

Obsessions

A man thinks about sex every fifteen seconds.
—George Carlin

i think about food
almost as often

the way a bagel tastes
in the morning

or the way
oreos taste in bed
at night

or even the way
your skin
is salty

which is really
two thoughts
at once

The Visit

this is my room

a table   a chair
a bed

a fruit basket
in the window

next to the electric razor
my daughter bought me

there's little to do
but look out the window

my clean room's
almost empty

my wishes end
in always

The Budget

my wife calls us
"involuntary vegetarians"

what she means is
these days
it is not steak
and lobster
but rice and salads

it is coffee
on the back porch
for dessert

it is playing cards
in the evening
and watching the stars
at night
to see how they
change in number

it is how things
lately are
in this vegetable world
that changes

with phone calls
and bill collectors
and sighs

Elegy

i spent part
of today

trying to remember
the taste

of coffee in my
father's house

the way it was
strong from

the four scoops
of off-brand

and how the
water held

the brackish taste
of copper

from the old pipes
fed by the well

Mercy

when you say
mercy
hold the word in your mouth
a moment

the weight is the weight
of a thousand pebbles
placed
one at a time
on your tongue

if you feel dizzy
let your hands
fall to
your sides

the birds
that gather darkness
may come
to rest there

The Advancement of Learning

i don't regret
any time
i've spent
staring out the window

nothing good
was ever learned
in a hurry

olson says

the simplest
things
    are always
last

the years it took
to learn to fish

to bait a hook
the proper
way

Found Object

Old note left in a winter coat pocket
What you meant to say
Given a chance

Packing Day

three days after the funeral
all of your possessions
fit into four boxes

the acquisitions of seventy years
take less than an hour to pack

the cardboard boxes
we use are from the liquor store
three blocks away

each box bears the name
of some scotch
or bourbon

though i never saw you drink
i'm sure you must have
when you were younger

i've heard stories

each of the boxes
is slightly larger than
a breadbox

none of them are
very heavy

if we drove the boxes
around all day
and then all day tomorrow
they would never grow any bigger

our loss would remain
more vast than any highway
larger even than
the four chambers of the heart

Self-Knowledge

there are words
that scare you

home   safe
always

those abstractions
just beyond
your fingertips

your hands are
shaped by hunger

so to know is
to touch

to taste is
even better

Poem Dictated at Kazansky's Deli

"when i lost my job
    my wife threw me out

friends took me in for a while
    first one then the other

later, i slept in my old buick
    and dreamed about gypsies

(backseats never sleep good
even in summer)

i ate one cheap meal a day
    at tom's diner on carson street

i was skinny back then
    and didn't need much

every day i read the want ads
    and when i finished them

i read through berrigan's *sonnets*
    and wrote notes on every page

brad let me shower at his apartment
    at least three times a week

it was on shower day that my luck changed
and someone finally hired me

i think of those days
    not as the bad old days

but in the same way i think of
    a childhood friend i lost touch with

someone who would be a stranger now
    if we passed on the street"

The Birthday Dream

there is always a train

you swear
that one of the
passengers

is your mother
dead now
for ten years

she sits next to
the first girl
you ever kissed

they talk
like old friends

they eat
from plates
filled

with roasted duck
and other

delicacies
you never tasted

even in your
dream
of feasts

Old Love Letters

the words are there from
another life

when your haircut was different
and different friends stood beside you

old attitudes   old gossip
some of the same concerns
and yet

those clothes don't fit
anymore

the memories are salted stones
in well worn pockets

the letters are part of the life
you forgot to bury

the goodbyes
you forgot to keep

Holes in a T-Shirt

you own so little
you are afraid to throw things away

the broken toaster is, somehow, valuable
those thin, crinkled-up shoes are kept for a little while still

what you do not have makes a world around you
all the birds sing loudly there

In the 8th Month

for Diane

always now, your body aches
with growth

each day
you rub your rounded stomach
and make a wish

you pace the house
check the closets

already, you count your breath

Miles Davis and the Art of Love

blow a horn
if you can

i can't and there's a reason
but "it's a long story
and not very
interesting"

in fact
let's not talk about
what we can't do
at all

as in
the way i can't help
stuttering
whenever you enter
a room

like that

love should always
riddle our speech

Last Light and Rain at the Window

this evening
i want nothing more than a cigarette
a bag of potato chips
a dill pickle
& the zen god of the lower case g

good scripture is too terse
for song
    what is known
can fit on a business card
the eye is often as wrong
as the head

Rosemary

during your "salad days"
as a journalist in chicago
you interviewed a whole family of mayors
then quit to homeschool your boys
well before that was the fashion

later, you opened a bookstore
where you sat at a corner desk
chain smoked and sweat
regardless of the weather

no trust funds protected you
against creditors

there was always, in your store,
the smell of cigarettes, old papers
and the popcorn you ate (with extra salt)
for lunch

you fixed the world's
worst coffee
and gladly bragged about it

you joked
you were never a cook
even in a past life

were you widowed
or divorced?

where was your first
hometown?

every year
there are fewer memories

every year
they grow less specific

your hoarse, stroked voice
the echo of an echo
within the ear

the long sold bookstore
now a pet shop
with a well-scrubbed smell

Poem Spoken by Thomas McGrath in a Dream

all this foolishness
about words—

the crows still circle
in the endless sky

the clouds are still
an entrance

to something
we are not part of

The Apprentice

even after
these many years
there is still
learning

　　-the hammer
finds the nail
all along
it was meant for-

on good days
there is
rest

Grief

days when all you do is
follow your shadow

when tomorrow is a well-plotted mystery
without a villain
or a crime

Running Through Spain

i keep no promises
at least to myself

i'll never finish war and peace

never buy an expensive
motorcycle
because i am too cheap
and, mostly, too poor

never run with the bulls
in pamplona
while wearing a stylish, black beret

never sing better about love than the spanish
who like to drink
and make love
more than they like to be chased by bulls

the least romantic part
of the idea of pamplona is the
actual running

you know what martin mull says

the problem with running
is the ice keeps falling out of
your glass

Fairy Tales, Fears and the Gymnastics of Love

in any fairy tale a large bird can say
beware of this and that

as someone who
often listens to large, talking birds
i am often afraid

the dark does not scare me
and snakes have never
occupied
even one of my dreams

but frogs-even the tiny tree frog-
make me sweat
worse than long distance running

also, i don't like flight attendants

i am not afraid of them
but i don't like them and that
has not been said enough
in poems

instead, we say that you are beautiful
or a beautiful fool

we give these two refrains
a million variations

as if we could not stand on our heads
and think
of anything else to say

The Church on the Corner

On my knees in prayer, I saw, out of the corner of
my eye, a gray cat walk down the center aisle. A small
wooden doll hung limply from its mouth. No one
else seemed to notice, though, all the while, birds sang
hosannas in the trembling balcony.

In Fear of Eviction

snowflakes fall past the window

you count them
erratically
your sum as random
as the snowfall

in a corner of the room
you sit and wait
for a knock
on the door

today is not a day
for small miracles

today you need
to squeeze
water from rock

you need to burn
shadows
against the cold

The Mermaids

they were perfect
in their confinement

the shoes might come off
and the socks
and the shirt
and, o yes, the bra

but the shorts
or the jeans
or the skirt
always stayed in place

the mermaids offered themselves
to boys cracking
against
the floor of manhood

they lived in the back seats of cars
and in upstairs bedrooms
and in basement laundry rooms
and, occasionally,
in some half-secluded field

the mermaids were there
for rushed, sweaty palms
and kisses
for thank yous
and o my god
for thank yous

Poem

mother called crows
nothing birds

because she did not love them

because she knew
the magic of naming
what she did
not love

Plenty of Quarters

Let's forget about what bills are due

What's paid and unpaid
What we owe to god, country and the old lady down
the stairs

Let's put all our past due notices aside
A medium size basket will hold them

There is sandwich meat in the refrigerator
And bread on the counter for tomorrow

There are enough quarters in the change jar
For a bottle of wine from the all night corner market

There are more quarters in the change jar
Than there are stars in tonight's cloudy sky

Conversation is almost
Always free

A walk to the store takes
Only a few minutes

If we leave now we can get back
Before the rain starts

South of Here

a christmas letter from a friend five hundred miles away
his year filled with sickness and an absence of travel

he gives thanks for the new year, that his health
like an old, haggard dog is back for a while

with his illness he gave up travel (even day trips)
though he once collected new places as some people collect rings

take out menus now litter his kitchen
(with leftovers he can him mix and match his food)

these days, he hunts and fishes when he wants
rides his bike beside the bumpy catawba river

in remission, but single and alone at fifty, he writes,
"there's a chance the next woman i meet will have wings"

The Poet's Book of Professions

The Banker Poet
Gives away short poems
Written on
The back of dollar bills

The Janitor Poet
Cleans up the mess
Of other poets

The Surgeon Poet
Leaves his poems inside his patients

The Academic Poet
Attaches footnotes to everything

The Clown Poet
Uses balloon animals
Even when
He shouldn't

The Postman Poet
Delivers his own rejection letters

The Porn Star Poet
Can recite her poems
In any position

The Performance Poet
Uses profanity as punctuation

The Professional Poet
Always gets paid
His pennies shine like the moon

The Baker Poet
Uses secret ingredients

The Fashion Model Poet
Never chooses
Meaty subjects

The FBI Poet
Writes from
The Witness Protection Program

The Accountant Poet
All of his poems
Operate at a loss

The Taxi Driver Poet
Has not yet been translated

The Truck Driver Poet
Poems decorate his mud flaps

The Car Dealer Poet
Gets high mileage
Out of every poem

The Director Poet
ZOOM IN

The Journalist Poet
Never gives a deadline
To the poem

The Chef Poet
Can recite poems
With a full mouth
(See also, porn star poet)

The NASCAR Driver Poet
His work loved
By speed readers everywhere

The Stripper Poet
Those aren't dollar bills
In her g-string

The Farmer Poet
Knows
Every poem
Is organic

The Engineer Poet
There's a straight line
In every poem

The Lawyer Poet
Define poem

The Eco-Poet
Writes only
In the air

The Dog Catcher Poet
Is sick of
Dead animal poems
Loves Judy Garland

The Political Poet
Every poem
A letter to the editor

The Unemployed Poet
Sorry, this is redundant

The Jazz Poet
Combine unemployed poet
With performance poet
Add alcohol

The Critic Poet
Never shows his poems

The Mobster Poet
Doesn't like criticism
Or your mother

The Magician Poet
The rabbit writes his poems

The Romantic Poet
Likes your mother
And your sister

The Window Washer Poet
Is John Bennett

The Librarian Poet
Lives inside her own joy

The Weatherman Poet
Knows every poem about a sunset
Still has
A chance of rain

Unlikely Things

if i put the world in a small box
i can figure it out

it's there to go back to
to pack and unpack

an odd collection of
drawings and photographs
letters and spare change

all the parts
good enough to save

and the parts
not even memory can
break down

to find a story in all the pieces
is not hard

the story is there in the deep stain of summer
and in the bare echo of winter

the hero is the fellow who walks backwards
with the mirror of splintered glass

In Fear of Collection Agencies

yesterday
they turned the power off

now
we are in the dark
together

a married couple
with

no lights
no matches
no lanterns
no wicks

canned food in the cabinets
wheat bread on the counter

the water still on

Carl's Tavern
for R.D. Armstrong

if this bar had a p.o. box
i could live here

almost everyone
says that

the local beer is cheap enough
for lint-filled pockets

every tuesday night there are
free wings

if you stay until closing time
you get a nickname

the neon sign in the window
always says, "come in"

Necessary Fictions

The invention of soft-serve ice cream
Would have changed the cavemen
And all those paintings they left us

And who would want that

Those paintings are wonderful
Each one like the work
Of a gifted child

It's probably not right to call the work
Of pre-literate people childish
But they will never read this

Those figurative paintings
As basic as black

The cavemen drew the eternals
Deer, fire, funerals
A trio that always goes together

The Other Country

for Jack Wolford
d. 12-16-2005

in your new country
every night is starless

there is only the still life
of dreams

Homemade Routines

for Michael Simms

i finished the last part of today's crossword puzzle
by throwing it in the trash

i need to waste some time every day
as surely as i need gossip and sandwiches

this morning i shaved at the sink
instead of in the shower

all day i've walked two steps slower than normal

too many days of this and my hair will grow long
i will begin to speak in riddles of broken syntax

too few days of this and not even my shadow
could find me beneath the sun

Last Poem

he wanted children in the hungry way
abraham did   so he had them

his children were numerous
clear-eyed and profound

of all the women there are to love
he had one   which was enough

all his life there were many friends
though some left early

his heart was large   but slow
everyone knew when he missed a beat

the things he knew were small
particular   but true

more than once he used
his loud voice to sing

Obituary

say nice things about me   jack said

tell everyone that i loved
black olives
sinclair lewis and the early work of
philip guston

my secrets were numerous and
avowedly profane

only once in my life did i quote
rick flair
(the greatest wrestler of all time)

the quote is in greek
and untranslatable

tell people i always said
what i thought
i never danced around a subject
like a bird around a tree

that's not true, but it is how
i would like to be remembered

surely, you can see that

Furnished Room

For Rick St. John

there's no good decoration
for a furnished room

no potted plant can lighten it

too much sleep doesn't make
the room brighter

too little sleep only darkens it

the stain on the carpet
is from someone else

the cigarette burns on the couch
aren't from your brand

there's a ring on the table
where you place your drink

the fingerprints on the window
are always there

Travels

more than anything you remember
the farmhouse

you walked through it
as though it were home

you expected people
in every room

you expected laughter
the clink of ice cubes on glass

instead, the rooms were empty
the wood floors swept clean

the house vacant except for a clock
left silent on a wall

First Poem in a New Town

we all need a place to sleep

where i've ended up is
not home, but
nearly

each day birds move the horizon
piece by piece

One Line Memoirs

Sought useless degrees, for no profit.

Believed Hawaiian shirts to be fashionable.

Disliked clubs. Never joined the military.

Lived next door to a mime.

Loved naked women most of all.

Didn't like hugs. Not one bit.

Started exactly sixteen novels and then…

More errands than time allowed for.

Could not paint, though wished to.

Always meant to do something else.

Collected people. Collected quotes from them.

Best friend died. Loneliness never did.

Wanted money, but never got it.

Thought ventriloquists made the best conversationalists.

Ate saltines in bed every night.

Never did laundry, even when asked.

Never learned to cook. Intended to.

Had lots of children. Then died.

Family Album

the old photographs are mostly grim

a dusty world of black iron stoves
bad coughs and grease fat

where no one smiles
or tries to

the only pose is a serious
bit-lip expression

as if each photograph is just another job
among the long lists of jobs

Boaz

the mountains are small
but keep you
in place

what you see beyond them
doesn't change

chance is your need

that prayer is the one
you missed

Once I Check Out of Here

look for me out beyond the fork in the woods
beside the last leaf on a stunted tree

i'll be disguised as a squirrel
so remember to dress like st. francis

if you bring your banjo
i promise not to dance

i promise to dance
if you sing

Fortune's Bitter Cookies

The friend who lent you money
would rather you stay away.

Your future is filled with
boring strangers.

There's not enough concrete
to bury all your mistakes.

Secretly, but on most days,
your dog doesn't like you.

The best advice is from dreams.
You are an insomniac.

The graffiti in the bathroom
mentions you by name.

When you stand in the shade
remember to stand still.

New Year's Poem for My Wife

My shoes can last a few more months

There's enough soap, enough spoons, enough blankets
There's even more than enough

So let's make what we can for dinner
From a box of this or that

Whatever we need is there for tomorrow
We know where tomorrow is

In a Gray Country
for Kell Robertson

the raven knew the shape of the heart
and stayed

so where do we go

the sky leads in one direction
but the cold river
pulls at our ankles

near the water
there is a horse

with some luck
we will guess his name

Dickey

old by then
more smiling, fleshy legend
than working writer

he liked to quote mozart
on the importance
of silence

he liked to quote
rilke   valery
robinson

he said poems
aren't like knick-knacks
placed on a shelf
for display

poems are like
furniture

couches and chairs

the objects we
live with
daily

he said
more than once
there's a music
in every word

he said
we only make choices
there are no wrong
words

Rightsizing

Give up extra bed, cable tv, strip mall clothes,
subscription to New York Times, new car thoughts,
vacations not on the cheap, shiny Christmas presents,
now and then gifts in April and June, savings account,
better schools, down the road retirement hopes

Not say goodbye to books, laughter, family, home
grown vegetables, children's drawings, conversations,
the radio, weekend sleep ins, friends, coffee, eternity

Postscript, Etc.

at night we shared our insomnia
over the phone

neither watched our words
nor counted the time

he told me
    he got eight hours sleep
an hour or two
here and there

with no "real job"
he made do

sold books and antiques

ghost wrote articles

worked a town fair, once,
as a ticket man

mainly, he drank coffee
and smoked hand-rolled cigarettes

mainly, he talked
and talked

his whole life filled with words
with what he meant to say

as there's always something else
as there's always one more thing

Fifteen Women Named Eva

That one has eleven toes, each painted red
That one hates her name
That one collects postcards from the world's most sacred spots
That one doesn't
That one married six times, is now a lesbian
That one reads chemistry textbooks for fun
That one wanted to be a doctor became a mortician
That one didn't start out as Eva
That one bets whatever she has
That one doesn't own a television, a camera or a computer
That one sleeps with the light and the radio on
That one loves turtles, hates birds
That one says, maybe, twenty words a day
That one learned French from her mother, Italian from her father
                                        before they divorced
That one holds her breath on elevators, spends lots of time
                                        outdoors

Refugees

this world is black and white

the line for bread goes
one way

the line for wool blankets
curls like a rope around a corner

we say thank you
for the tin cups

we know that somewhere
on a general's shelf

a jar is filled
with gold teeth

In a Photograph, from Africa

a crouched child
      hugs his thin legs
            with his thin arms

    opens his mouth
        but not to speak

near the child
    there is one tree
       bare and black

one tree   no grass   lots of sun   no weeds

beside the tree
     to the left
        there is a vulture

there is only one reason he is there

Poem

who knows the names of flowers
not us

these are fresh picked
yellow and common

they may be daisies
so we call them that

if we are wrong, then we have
our own language to
be wrong in

ah, well

there's a copper vase for them
in the kitchen window

the vase needs to be polished
it's been that way for a while

The Past

is the house we leave in the dark
and drive away from
in the rain

every road washes out
just after we cross it

as if all sentences end
in goodbye

Cowboys

You could dam a river with those big hats they wear
Then swim away to the other side
Then start all over again
And make a farm that is just yours
Where even the rose bushes become familiar

Adam Lived Longer than Eve

each morning he woke with an ache in his ribs
then touched where she had been

he traced his scar with the lone compass of his fingers
but found no good map within his dreams

Leftovers Mean Abundance

Leftovers mean abundance.

The last three bites of a ham sandwich
on a plate
at an all night diner.

That image:
"one of the clichés you love."

Everything is used up
with a cliché.

Jack Wolford

What of the book addled poet who shared my town?

What of his single necktie? The cotton, blue one?

What of his breath that could fill a steamboat?

What of black coffee insomnia conversations?

What of him who ate vienna sausages with gusto?

What of cigarette burns on bent couches?

What of concrete park benches freckled with pigeon droppings?

What of guttural Spanish in bleary, profane dreams?

What of the river that turned crystal at night?

What of his ink stained fingers?

What of his jar of pens?

1945-2005

Rorschach Test

When his hands
made
shadow puppets
he only saw
alligators.

He even saw their teeth.

There Are So Few Facts

there are so few facts
about margaret

each one   simple   basic

   —black ink
on a white
page—

when she was born
who she married

   —some say
the world lasted
longer then

Far North

if there's no god we won't know
what we miss

say that ten times fast

close your eyes and think of
the first prayer you ever said

think of the way you held
your hands then

Objects

he said i would love to own
an old cigar box guitar

but
i said
you don't play guitar
you barely listen to music
you turn the radio on
maybe
once a week

i don't want to play it
he said
i want to hang it on my wall
one of those guitars
doesn't have to be played
think of how those old guitars look

Growing Older

Suddenly, ear hairs require grooming

Identifying a Suspect out of a Line Up at Police Headquarters

Yes, that is the one
The man in the pink panties
The fellow who looks like Hemingway in drag
I can't be certain about his face
But the birthmark on his upper right arm
The one in the shape of Mt. Rushmore
I would know that anywhere

And So, Sometimes, Horizons Change

A man goes out to get the newspaper from his driveway
But walks past the newspaper
Past the mailbox
Walks down the sidewalk out of his neighborhood
Leaves his favorite cereal in his breakfast bowl
And the jar of quarters beside his computer
And the wind up clock in the hall closet
And the address book full of birthdays, thank yous and goodbyes
The man ignores his neighbors and their cars
He does not think of daily commutes or taxes
He thinks of his walk and the shape of the road
He thinks of his legs and how they feel
As he remembers his life
As he forgets it

The Witch Long Dead, Hansel and Gretel Return to the Forest

the house is gone

they stand in the old woods
facing north
among trees planted
years before
they came

their feet are bare and there's no path
just pine needles on the ground

no breadcrumbs today
for one another and the birds

no white pebbles
to reflect the light

they talk less
than ever
there's no because
for that

no matter where they look
the house is gone

Derringer

for Thomas Lux

A pistol designed by Henry Deringer (who died
of natural causes,
age 81, in 1868) was renowned throughout
the late 1800's.

Considered a great gift for assassins, such
as John Wilkes Booth
(who used his for noted effect),
as well as for ladies of all varieties.

The derringer (two r's)
is known as a "muff shot", a "purse gun" and
a "garter pistol."

In the twentieth century it became a favorite
of both Kenny Rogers (singer/chicken entrepreneur/
noted gambler) and of Elvis Aaron Presley (The once
and always king of rock-n-roll.
Thank you very much.)

Early derringers could only fire
one shot,
but thanks to those forever advances in
the gunsmith trade
later versions were able to fire two.

If you said such a small gun
is not effective
at close range
you'd be stone dead wrong.

The Aptly Named Visitor

he came for the blueberry pancakes
and he stayed
and stayed
and breakfast and lunch were both over and he was still there
and we thought of giving him a blanket and a place on the couch
while we went out for a walk in the park on what was really a
lovely spring day
but then he rose from the table and cleared his throat
and said, "the news doesn't make itself"
no, no it never does
so he left for his place and we stayed where we were
and we did not take a walk on that day or the next
and the spot on the couch remained
unblanketed and cool

Versions

those stories we edit for children
about our younger selves

about who we met
or almost met

about the city we almost moved to
the one near the beach on the other coast

about the person we almost married
the person we think of each january

about light on dusty tables in long gone houses
and where the tables came from and the houses went

about wood fires in black stoves
and meals no one eats much anymore

all those things from the days
before we became as old as now

I Used to Dream of Becoming the Village Idiot

For Charles Bukowski

The children would toss apples at me
And I would eat the apples

Sometimes I would take the apples
To a kind matron
(A blacksmith's wife)
She would bake me an apple pie

No one would throw the apple pie at me
I would eat all of it
Alone
Beneath a tree
In a field far away from the children

At night the stars would stay in place
Not even the wind would make them blink

After One Thousand Rejection Letters I Wrote this Poem Above a Public Urinal

goodbye ambition
now is the time to settle in
be comfortable and dry
see the world as it is

depressed by love or by state
the old chinese poets
went to the drunken river and
made boats of their poems

then set fire to the boats
as they watched them sail away

Clouds and Bad Coffee

my father visits
in a dream

he looks tired
more tired than the
last time

his brown glasses
are cracked in one corner

he wants to talk

ask me anything
he says

so what's it like over there

cold, he says, always cold
except when it rains
which doesn't happen often

there's really
not very much to do
he says

we pace a lot and
watch the sky

plus the coffee isn't
very good
a good cup of coffee is rare

a real treat, he says,
a real treat